OTHER BOOKS BY PATRICK HICKS

FICTION
The Commandant of Lubizec:
A Novel of the Holocaust and Operation Reinhard

POETRY
This London
A Harvest of Words (editor)
Finding the Gossamer
The Kiss that Saved My Life
Draglines
Traveling Through History

Praise for Adoptable

"Adoptable *is a tender, hopeful book of a father's observational grace. A heartwarming gift from the poet to his young son, this book bursts with love while knowing that 'at the heart of very adoption...is a breaking apart.' From South Korea to South Dakota, these touching poems offer an accurate window into the experience of fatherhood and adoption. The son's bright light shines on each and every page, and just as Hicks hopes his son will one day find 'the galaxy widening before him,' readers of this book will discover the same: a galaxy in the poet's love for his son. These poems, this poet, this son— treasures that will expand your heart.*"

LEE HERRICK, author of *Gardening Secrets of the Dead*

"Adoptable *is a powerful and moving book of poems by Patrick Hicks that focuses on the adoption of a Korean child and the way the narrator and his wife become as connected to this child as any birth parent possibly could be. These poems are lyrical praise songs to the family relationship that emerges and to the power of love. The poems are perfectly crafted and the endings simply lift off the page. Hicks is an amazing and exquisite poet.*"

MARIA MAZZIOTTI GILLAN, American Book Award winner

"'*At the heart of every adoption is a ripping, a knifepoint, a breaking apart, / like cracking open an oyster*" writes Patrick Hicks in his stunningly moving new collection, Adoptable. *These poems ride that knifepoint edge into the vulnerable center of the poet's experience adopting his Korean-born son, Sean Min-gyu, with raw honesty and humble compassion. Adoptable explores the complexities of adoptive diaspora in deft language of fierce silver clarity, wit, and unabashed tenderness—a father's poems written in an adopted tongue to hold and encircle his beautiful boy with the twice-cut umbilical cord, and to inscribe the kind of love so big it reaches across borders, across oceans, across time.*"

LEE ANN RORIPAUGH, author of *Dandarians*

"'*And when you find me,'* Patrick Hicks writes, *of playing hide-and-seek with his young son, 'it is like a lock clicking open.' This wonder—it's ours, too, as Hicks clicks open the locks of the human heart in his latest, loveliest collection,* Adoptable, *in which, like the heart, we find wide, wind-swept rooms of kindness, humor, grief, worry, confusion, and—most especially—of the good luck of being alive, of stunned, staggering wonder.*"

JOE WILKINS, author of *The Mountain and the Fathers*

Adoptable
Patrick Hicks

Author of
THE COMMANDANT OF LUBIZEC

salmonpoetry

Published in 2014 by
Salmon Poetry
Cliffs of Moher, County Clare, Ireland
Website: www.salmonpoetry.com
Email: info@salmonpoetry.com

Copyright © Patrick Hicks, 2014

ISBN 978-1-908836-82-3

COVER IMAGE: "Painted by Spring" by Andreja Hojnik Fišić
COVER DESIGN & TYPESETTING: *Siobhán Hutson*
Printed in Ireland by Sprint Print

Salmon Poetry gratefully acknowledges the support of
The Arts Council / An Chomhairle Ealaoín

for Sean Min-gyu,

of course

Publication Credits

America: "The Poet Laureate of North Korea"

Atlanta Review: "Speechless"

Clackamas Literary Review: "Hide-and-Seek"

Cold Mountain Review: "Umbilical Cord," "Mother's Day," and "When He is an Old Man"

Commonweal: "Adults Only" (Cover story, printed as "Family Planning")

Comstock Review: "Read This"

Korean Quarterly: "I Believe" and "Is/Was"

Levure Littéraire: "Flutter," "Ghost," and "Delicate"

Natural Bridge: "Balloon"

Paddlefish: "The Essential Glossary to Adoption", "Summer in January", and "Adoptable"

Paterson Literary Review: "Listening to John Lennon's Greatest Hits" and "Sleeping in My Childhood Bedroom".

Poetry City USA: "The Strangers" Minneapolis: Lowbrow Press, 2011

Toad Suck Review: "Watching M*A*S*H," "Border Crossing," "Seoul Man," and "The Task List"

Acknowledgments

When I was growing up, I didn't think much about adoption. But now that I'm sliding into middle age, and I'm raising an energetic little boy, I'm aware that I've joined a very wide and diverse community. Adopting a child is like opening a secret door to elsewhere. I had no idea that so many people have been touched by adoption, and as I continue to learn more about being a father, I also realize that adoption stories have two essential components: longing and belonging. As my son grows up, I hope he knows that we have loved him powerfully and that we have tried to see his existence in America through his eyes. He will have questions. He will want answers. And I look forward to listening to him. More than anything, I look forward to watching him grow into himself.

Until then, I am unfairly blessed with family and friends who have helped me understand fatherhood, Korea, adoption, and poetry much better. Many of them have made this book stronger. So thank you Jeffrey Miller, Barb Ebeling, Nick Hayes, Lee Herrick, Irene Chang, Jim Reese, Brian Turner, Lee Ann Roripaugh, Joe Wilkins, Siobhán Hutson, Stephen Wunrow, Sheila Risacher, Erin Crowder, Jayson Funke, Lynne and Jim Hicks, and my wonderful wife, Tania. Many thanks also to Andreja Hojnik Fišić for allowing me to use her stunning artwork, "Painted by Spring" for the cover—all that vibrant color splashed onto a blue background is a wonderful visual metaphor for what it's like to be a parent. I owe a huge debt of thanks to Jessie Lendennie at Salmon Poetry. Where would my writing career be without the chance you took on my work ten years ago?

And lastly, I want to thank my son, Sean Min-gyu. You have no idea how much greater and more beautiful my life has become because of you. You are sunshine. You are light.

Contents

Morning

The Strangers

on the night my internationally adopted son arrived

After we picked you up at the Omaha airport,
we clamped you into a new car seat
and listened to you yowl
beneath the streetlights of Nebraska.

Our hotel suite was plump with toys,
ready, we hoped, to soothe you into America.
But for a solid hour you watched the door,
shrieking, *Umma*, the Korean word for mother.

Once or twice you glanced back at us
and, in this netherworld where a door home
had slammed shut forever, your terrified eyes
paced between the past and the future.

Umma, you screamed. *Umma!*
But your foster mother back in Seoul never appeared.

Your new mother and I lay on the bed,
cooing your birth name,
until, at last, you collapsed into our arms.

In time, even terror must yield to sleep.

Umbilical Cord

When you arrived from South Korea,
the adoption agency sent over your umbilical cord.
This purple stump, shriveled like a raisin,
is clasped in a plastic vice—

its jawed teeth bite down on that moment
when you were snipped away
from your birth mother.

For almost a year it has followed you from
hospital to orphanage to foster home,
then across the wide Pacific to our little house.

It nuzzles in the attic now, waiting,
waiting, I suppose, until you find it as a man,
and study its wrinkled shape. This dried root

binds you to a moment of loss, it is a gap
between two different worlds: both here
and there.

Seoul Man

From the very beginning you've been called
"Choe Min-gyu" by your birth mother,
"K2009-0439" by the adoption agency,
and "Sean Min-gyu Hicks" by us, your parents.
This final name is permanent—
or as permanent as words can ever be.

In our nine months together,
an unexpected gestation has occurred
where nicknames are attached to you one day,
then shucked off the next.

We call you The Boy, Poopy McScreamy,
Diaper Destroyer, Mr Puke, Sir Grunts-a-lot,
The Total Package, The Streak, The Peeing Machine,
Genghis Sean, The Screamin' Korean. Seoul Man.

These English words mark you only because
you were plucked from your native soil
and, sometimes, as I hold you against my shoulder,
I wonder about your birth mother.

Does her voice still echo in your ear,
like the sea in a conch shell?

Do you still hear the murmur of her tongue?
In your dreams, does she whisper your first name?

Balloon

after Sylvia Plath

Since April you have lived with us,
scooting around the house,
exploring the carpets as your own.
I got a *Welcome Home* balloon—
one of those mylar ones
that never seem to deflate or shrivel.
For two months it has ghosted from room
to room, migrating on heat currents.

Most mornings you yank on its string
like a medieval bell ringer.

And so, I shouldn't have been surprised
to watch you wheel down the heavens,
hug this silver globe close to your chest
and then, as if it were a shiny pillow,
leap against the floor, laughing.

I expected a rifle shot—

                    a bang

but you bounced off,
you, of such little weight,
and the balloon floated up,
back to its cockeyed perch.

There was no silver shred in your fist,
no lost innocence, no tears.

Ignoring me,
you tugged the balloon back down,
held it in your little hands,
and—while laughing—began to bite.

Listening to John Lennon's Greatest Hits

—December 8, 2010

It has been thirty years
since he hemorrhaged outside the Dakota,
      his glasses misted with blood,

but tonight his voice floats around the house
as we play with trucks and dinosaurs.

I am now the same age he was
when a .38 Special
opened its oiled mouth.

As one song ends, another begins.

"Beautiful boy," he sings, and I lean
into my own son, my own Sean—
"beautiful, beautiful, beautiful,
      beautiful boy."

I don't hear a Beatle, not today.
Today, I hear a father like me,
glowing with incandescent love.

This is how time can twist itself,
how one life can echo into another,
how thirty orbits of the Earth

can find John and I singing together
in praise of fatherhood—
"beautiful, beautiful, beautiful,
      beautiful boy."

Speechless

His tongue is greeting words
that will become friends for a lifetime—
words like *ball*, *dog*, and *juice*.

He tilts his head at *please*,
points at *trucks* on the highway,
and it was my own mother who taught him *more*.

It took fifteen minutes of work,
but I gave him *no*,
which, in hindsight, I regret,

especially when he trumpets that word around the house
and runs away from me at bath time.

Yes has come more slowly to him,
as it does for us all.

When he falls asleep in the chair
of my body, I sometimes wonder about
the history of my own language.

How was it that words like
moonlight and *firmament* and *campfire*,
as ancient as *petroglyphs* to me now,
how were they first painted onto my tongue?

When my son stirs because a car backfires,
I squint into his mouth and realize
someone will teach him the sour words
of *betrayal*, and *deceive*, and *fuck*.

There will be others who give him *fart* and *wedgie*.

Someone too—ah, this will be sweet for him—
someone too will cup his face,
and kiss him lightly on the lips.

Her words will be so humid and tropical
it will feel like a brand new language.

And in this moment,
I hope he is *tongue-tied, dumbstruck,
inarticulate*, speechless.

Surprising Things I Have Said

Toilet paper is for people, not dinosaurs.

Coffee cups are *not* shoes. Take those off your feet.

Stop licking the wall.

Stop licking the cell phone.

Stop licking the television.

Did you shove a pea up your nose?

Don't wipe boogers on my cookie.

Stop biting my pocket.

I don't care if you're a dinosaur, it's still bed time.

Put your underwear on. Then we'll talk.

Dirt is an outside toy.

The sun? The sun is a star that's very close to us. It's our home star. It's a big bubble of burning gas.

"Trees" are what we call them when they're alive. "Wood" is what we call them when they're dead. Furniture is made out of dead trees.

If you can't get out of your house, it's called a "prison".

Look, I can touch vomit, but you can't.

Soup is not finger-paint.

For the last time, take that plastic bag off your head.

Don't sit in the fridge.

I eat books with my eyeballs and put them in the tummy of my head.

Don't ride that jar of mustard around the kitchen. Mustard is not a car.

If you're alive, you can move.
If you're dead, you can't.

This is important. Are you listening to me? It's okay to be scared. It's what you do *because* you're scared that really matters. Do you do nothing, or do you something? And let me tell you . . . you're smart. You can do anything.

Watching *M*ᐟ*A*ᐟ*S*ᐟ*H*

When I was a kid, I focused on the O.R.
and how Hawkeye used words like *flange*,
and *hemostat*, and *chest-splitter*.
Soldiers were served up beneath his scalpel—
they were peeled open like TV dinners.

Thirty years later,
Korean orphans are still trucked into the 4077th.
There are so many huddled around Father Mulcahy
that I jump into the television to find my son.
I no longer care about seeing the Swamp
or lounging around in a Hawaiian shirt.

      I only want my boy.

He is on the edge of camp, near a mine field,
and I bring him to the mess tent
where I feed him powdered eggs and liver.

Klinger asks if I want a different boy.
"Take your pick," he says. "We got a thousand of 'em."

It makes me wonder about the bureaucrat,
the one who stapled our names together in Seoul.
Did she shuffle a stack of paperwork,
and make us father and son before going to lunch?

Back on television, Radar yells out, "We got choppers!"

As metallic dragonflies skim over a mountaintop,
American boys will soon arrive into camp, bloody
and broken.

How little I know of this war.

And yet, I have been watching it on rerun
all my life.

Border Crossing

The ceiling fan above me is a motionless X,
a type of cancellation as my wife is down the hall,
sleeping on the floor with our boy.
They say this will soothe his transition into America,
but the distance   between our rooms
is like salt water taffy, a resin of time zones.

He bleats into the dark, and I'm reminded
that South Korea is fourteen hours ahead of us.
The DMZ bristles with barbed wire, and his birth
country is split across the middle, divided,
as if by King Solomon.

Staring down the hallway,
I imagine my wife tip-toeing back to our bedroom.
She lets her clothes fall in a pool of fabric.
The moons of her breasts are lit by the doorway
and, as she crawls on top of me, our tongues
rediscover the lost maps of our bodies.

His shriek is an illumination flare,
and she circles back, cooing his name.

The X above me floats,
a ghostly breeze spins it to a +

So it goes with all borders that are crossed:
cancellation and addition.

The Task List

is never done because there are always
toys to clean up and soiled diapers and
dishes and bottles and floors, and there is a
grocery list to edit even during your naps
when Chopin lullabys the house, there is a
checkbook to balance and phone calls to
make where adults tap out the Morse
Code of a distant world full of exotic
travel, champagne, and dinner parties,
which makes me feel like a miner trapped
in a coal seam, my world is a
straightjacket of five rooms and I wonder
what became of my younger self, that
man who glowed in Barcelona and made
love in ski chalets, he is just a ghost as I
tick off line, after line, after line, after line,
of the task list, hoping to write through
your naps and, sometimes, when you're
fast asleep, I want to worm into your skull
to find out if you dream of South Korea,
of the ghosts you left behind, and maybe
the cherry blossoms are fluttering down
like all these receipts for baby monitors
and formula are fluttering down around
me now, and maybe, just maybe, you're
looking up at the trees and thinking about
how beautiful it all is even as I squint into
the sun—my coal miner's helmet dusted
with midnight— and I blink at the vast
open sky. I come up for air. I breathe
deep. I exhale. I relax. That's when the
task list yawns awake and I climb into the
bucket, going down down down, back
into the great maw of its throat

Seeing

It seemed a strange phobia,
how you turned away from owls,

how you refused to sleep
if a teddy bear stared at you.

     "Eyes," you said. "Me see eyes."

They are hatches to our souls,
the twinned periscopes of the brain.

These bubbles of egg white
are the meeting points

between the world beyond us,
and the lightning inside our minds.

They allow words to rise from the page
and nest in the skull.

They are portholes
to something deep and grand.

Maybe I'm seeing this fear all wrong,
but I know this much:

one day you were in South Korea,
and then you were in South Dakota.

Everyone in your new family had alien eyes,
we floated towards your crib at night.

How else can a two-year-old process such change?

     "Eyes. Me see eyes."

And so, at bedtime,
I turn the teddy bear around,
knowing that, when you're older,

racists will turn from you,
all because of eyes.

Sleeping in My Childhood Bedroom

In the fog between waking and dreaming,
my wife becomes a mermaid,
her arm is castaway
on the island of my chest.

The hothouse flower of our son
is asleep in a crib.
A sound machine is set to *Ocean*,
and laughing seagulls drift across the bed.

A younger me is ghosting around this room,
making model airplanes, reading dictionaries,
mapping the future, meditating
on the religion of breasts.

The life jacket of my suitcase
rests near the door.

Once, I floated away from this place,
wandered as aimless as Odysseus—
my compass wobbly, the rudder my own—
and I met my wife near the sea.
A squall of sperm carried our boy into this room,
where, now, he snores softly in the dark.

Waves froth around the raft of our bed,
and we drift out into an uncharted world.

At 40, I thought my adventures were all behind me,
but, oh irony, I see now they are just beginning.

Pancakes

I love how you fissure open an egg,
how your little nails pierce the shell.

I'm amazed how gentle you are,
how the yolk plops out, into flour.

We make smiley faces on the griddle—

       eye   eye

           grin

and then, a smothering of batter.

You clap, already reaching
for the blueberries,
which will become a nose,
or a goatee, or glasses.

We watch the edges bubble
and crisp.

When we flip this coin of breakfast
you shout, "I see a face!"

We are mixing your childhood,
pouring it into memory so that,
decades from now, in another life,

when you're a father yourself,
you can pull out baking soda,
line up the eggs, and bend low
into your child's ear.

Perhaps then you'll see how the ordinary
can crack open with beauty.

Is/Was

Yesterday, or the day before,
someone asked if my son was adopted.

Such a simple question, so easy,
but my tongue became quicksand.

Is adoption in the past—a *was*
       or is it forever ongoing—an *is*?

Legally it's over, the paperwork is dusty,
but my boy will always have questions
about Korea, and home, and belonging.

Emotionally, it never ends,
it is stuck in the present tense.

The question was repeated,
       "Hey buddy, was your kid adopted?"

I nodded, searching the compass points
between is and was.

How do you describe something
so vast, so deep, so complicated?

It's like holding water in your hands
and then explaining what the ocean is
to someone who has never seen it.

Mother's Day

Your second birthday happened
to fall on the day we celebrate maternal love.
We had a party to honor your 730 days of life,

and I, thinking of your birth mother—
that seventeen-year-old girl who might be chewing gum
or texting her friends in Cheongju—

I wanted to honor her. She must wonder
what corner of the planet you fell upon,
so I got a sumptuous dark cupcake,

something fancy with a raspberry on top,
and I thought about giving it to you
with your T-Rex birthday cake.

In this way, she might join us
because (and I must say this) I am thankful
every day for the warm galaxy of her body.

As I drove home from the bakery,
with the egg of a cupcake
safely protected in a womb of plastic,

the writer in me imagined a poem
where you would take your dinosaur cake
and squeeze it around this token of richness.

Your little hands would knead the chocolate,
bind it as one, and you would eat fistful after fistful,
filling up your belly with the past and the present.

Yes, I smiled. A good poem. A good day.

But when I got home and showed the cupcake
to your mother, your everyday mother,
the woman who holds you at midnight,

    she winced, and left the room.

I knew then that I'd misjudged
the power of chocolate and memory.
There can only be one mother on Mother's Day,
even though you will always have two—

    one seen, the other hidden.

Nap Time

Adults Only

Winter 2007

I've been getting a lot of sex lately. Back when I was randy teenager this would have seemed like an impossible dream-come-true, but now that I'm in my late thirties, and my wife and I are still trying to fill our empty nursery, it's a bit soul-crushing. Where is our first child, the one who throws cereal on the floor and cries at night and gets excited about opening Christmas presents? Where is this little phantom that we have imagined for so many years?

It never occurred to me that I couldn't be a father. I just assumed it was a rite of passage that I would embrace when my life was ready for it. Back when I was going through puberty, fatherhood was something that I wanted to avoid until I had a career and other grown-up accessories like a red sports car, but I never dreamed that becoming a father would be denied to me. The nuns in my Catholic school made it seem like I only had to unhook a woman's bra and my wandering sinful fingers would take care of the rest. Sperm was powerful stuff that should be locked away inside my testicles where it belonged. According to these nuns, getting a girl pregnant was dangerously easy. But they lied to me. It's not easy. It's not easy at all.

There are currently six million couples in the United States who stare into an empty nursery and wonder what is wrong with their bodies. Infertility, which has been on the rise over the past several decades, is generally defined as the inability to conceive after twelve months of unprotected sex. My wife and I have been trying now for forty-two months and we get tight-lipped whenever we see advertisements for diapers or toys or family vacations. We notice when the rabbits in our backyard have produced yet another bumper crop of bunnies.

Tania and I met in our late twenties. We both led bohemian lifestyles and spent our post-college years wandering the planet and living in a number of exotic countries. We met on a busy street in England, we started talking to each other, and we decided to grab a sandwich at a café. Since that day we have been devoted to each other. It was love at first sight, just like a sappy romantic comedy where love blossoms between an American and an Englishwoman. That chance meeting in July (the odds are stupidly high that we should be together at all) tugged us towards a new adventure in Barcelona. We shared our lives in that magnificent Spanish city and then got married in England. My bride packed her suitcase, immigrated to the United States, and we set about the business of having children. The nursery was ready, and so were we.

Giving a sperm sample is an unbelievably surreal experience. You stand in a cramped doctor's office as nurses flit outside your door talking to each other about their weekends, and there is a stack of porn on the counter. You stare at the slender glass jar in your hands, triple-check that you've locked the door, and then you unzip your pants.

I remember staring at the ceiling and shaking my head. How had it come to this?

After years of trying, we decided to have our reproductive organs checked out. We had already cut down on wine and caffeine. I was working out again. Tania took prenatal vitamins and she was charting the rhythm of her ovulation. We had relations—as our self-help book called it—at the right time of the month, but still nothing. Month after month of nothing.

Male virility is so much a part of manhood in our society that I began to feel inadequate, I began to feel like I was letting Tania down. I'd see ads with strong men flexing their biceps and I'd begin to wonder if, as the popular saying goes, I was shooting blanks. How would I feel if one of the trademarks of being a man in Western society was denied me? As I looked at the ceiling in the doctor's office I tried to imagine the microscopic world that was hidden deep inside my body. In the warm darkness of my epididymis, sperm were huddled and vibrating with eager life. They carried the blueprint of the future, and I hoped that they moved quickly enough, that their little tails were whipping the darkness at the right speed. When I was finished with the glass jar, I washed my hands and went back to work.

I had it easy though. I might have blushed as I sat in the waiting room for "Reproductive Endocrinology & Infertility" but at least I didn't have tubes and metal gadgets inserted into me. Our doctor, a Texan not much older than ourselves, recommended that Tania have something called a hysterosalpingogram. This meant she had to put on a flimsy hospital robe, climb onto a table, and spread her legs. A mildly radioactive dye would be injected through her cervix so that her uterus and fallopian tubes could be viewed. Any blockage or deformity could easily be spotted.

Tania held my hand as our doctor rummaged around in her privates. Even though it was all strictly very medical, it was still strange watching another man touch my wife down there. He grabbed a tube that he had earlier described as being "very thin" but it was the size of my pinky and it looked cold. Iodine was splashed onto everything. The red disinfectant made the table and instruments look so bloody that, if I didn't know better, I'd swear that Tania had just given birth to twins.

Our doctor was chatty and pleasant, and to my male eyes the procedure didn't seem to hurt too much. Tania squeezed my hand whenever there was a jolt of pain. We smiled at this because it was easy to imagine that we might be doing this for real in ten or eleven months. We both looked at her belly and I thought about taking Lamaze classes. Push, I wanted to say. You're doing fine, I wanted to say. Breathe.

When the dye was finally injected into Tania's body, the x-ray made her uterus and fallopian tubes turn black. All three of us looked at the monitor as if we were watching a moon landing.

"Your uterus, that's this thing here," our doctor said, tapping the screen, "looks fine. Same for your tubes. I don't see any leakage or blockage."

He spoke in a secret code of numbers to an attending nurse while Tania and I continued to stare at the monitor. There, in black-and-white, was a tiny sack of flesh no bigger than a matchbox. And yet, if we were lucky enough to have a child, that's where it would grow, that's where a tiny brain and heart would weave together. Tania squeezed my hand again, and we went home that night for a candlelight dinner.

I'd like to say we got pregnant and walked into the sunset with a biological child, but that would be a lie. Each month we kept on trying and each month our little world collapsed when tiny spots of menstrual blood appeared. Tania got depressed. I got depressed. And then her cycle began again and we tried harder and we hoped that maybe this time things would be different and then, just when it looked like we might become parents—

It's hard to stay positive after three years of failed babymaking, especially when we spent thousands of dollars to learn that our bodies are just fine. There is no reason we can't have biological children and, statistically speaking, we should already be parents by now. I used to think that I'd be happy to know that my seminal vesicles and vas deferens and all the other fleshy machinery inside of me worked as they should, but that's not the case. If anything, it makes it more frustrating because that big question—why can't we have kids?—hangs over us in a way it never did before we were poked and prodded by fertility specialists. We're both in our late thirties and if we got pregnant tomorrow the doctors would refer to us as having a "geriatric pregnancy". All of this makes me feel like I'm letting my family lineage down, and I know that Tania wonders if she will ever experience a life growing inside her. We both deal with our emotions of gender and expectation by talking to each other and being open with anyone foolish enough to ask why we don't have kids. Our closest friends know all about our adventures with medicine. Why be embarrassed about infertility? It's not our fault we can't have kids.

We've thought about doing in-vitro fertilization but that can cost over $15,000 and, at a lowly 15% success rate, it isn't much better than the old-fashioned way of getting knocked up. We're just not the gambling type. I have visions of being at a glitzy table in Las Vegas, dice in our hands, and we roll them down the velvet shoot. A doctor stands at the other end with our swaddled child. Tania and I watch the cubes tumble, bounce, roll, hop, trip, and eventually come to rest. I watch our faceless child being taken away and the chips of our money being scooped up by a hospital administrator.

On the other hand, adoption costs around $20,000 but it has a 100% success rate. A colleague of mine has two beautiful daughters from China. A friend of mine has two daughters from India. The more we talk about adoption, the more we like the idea of becoming a truly international family. I'm an American with Irish citizenship, Tania is English, and our son will be from...well, we're not sure yet. All of this appeals to me because I like the idea of bringing a new culture towards us, of grafting yet another country onto my soul, of surrounding a dispossessed little boy with love and opportunity.

The adoption application arrived yesterday and we're going to mail it off sometime next week. I just hope that, years from now, if my adopted son ever reads this, I hope he doesn't feel as if he were a second choice. True, this isn't the path we thought we'd take, but that's the mystery of life—it's open-ended and it nudges you in directions you couldn't possibly imagine. My life changed forever on a July afternoon in 1999 when I met Tania on a busy street in the UK. I didn't plan on falling in love with a non-American, I didn't plan on moving to Barcelona with her, but now I can't imagine my life without her. Who would have thought my wife would be English? I certainly didn't. Is it really so impossible to believe that my son might come from another country too?

It would be nice to offer a tidy ending to this story but it's only going to get more complicated and magnificent when we put a stamp on that adoption application. I'm not sure how everything will unfold, but I know this much: We're ready to love a child. We're ready for him to turn our lives upside down and bump us towards a glorious new adventure. We're ready for scrapped knees and sleeplessness nights and worry and laughter and birthdays and report cards. I hope he comes soon.

We've been waiting a long time for you, little one.

The Essential Glossary to Adoption

Adoption
> Making a child who is not biologically related to you, legally related to you.

Adoptee
> A child brought into a family. In the case of international adoptions, many non-white children are raised in white families. This often makes it hard to negotiate one's place in the world because parents and extended family members do not see this issue of racial minority, but others will when the child enters school and the workforce.

> Someone who belongs to two places at the same time. A lasting rupture. Home is not fastened deep in the soil; it wanders between time zones. Questions fog the world. Adoptive parents can never truly understand what this means—all they can do is listen, be supportive, and watch their child journey into the dark, shining a flashlight. This is the reality of taking a human being away from where they were born and transplanting them into a new world. For adult adoptees, some questions may never be answered. *Adoptee*: someone deeply beloved, but on a hard inward journey.

Agency
> An office that finds permanent homes for children; a place that binds strangers together for life. It is full of file cabinets, photos, documents, and hope.

Birth Name
> A hush of vowels and consonances; a whisper of cultural identity; a voice from the past. The tongue of the birth mother as she names her child. This word might be whispered into the dark, decades later, when she wonders what has become of her flesh and bone. For adoptive parents, this first name often becomes a middle name. It is to be honored. It is a password to the beginning.

Fee

A tally of all financial burdens incurred for taking care of a child prior to adoption. This includes all diapers, food, bottles, blankets, nurses, shots, x-rays, transportation, toys, photographs, taxes, medical exams, and foster care that took place before the child was given a permanent home. Not to be mistaken as the "price" for adopting a child or the value of a human life in general. It is a sum of what it has cost to keep the child healthy prior to life with a new family. Importantly, this isn't what a child costs; it is the cost of taking care of a child.

Gotcha Day

The day a child is given into your care. A type of (re)birthday that is both a beginning and also a separation from all that existed before. A gateway from one life to the next. Legal forms are signed and a child goes home with you. It can take place in a Chinese orphanage, in a lawyer's office, in a hospital room, or at regional airport in Nebraska. As a parent, you will be scared. You will be petrified. You will be joyful. A human life has been entrusted into your arms. Celebrate this day annually. With cake.

Home Study

A Social Worker shines a headlamp into the private corners of your life. Cobwebs are examined. Notes are scribbled onto legal paper and it feels like an interrogation. You will squirm in your seat. Background checks are done. The FBI is called. You are stripped financially naked. However, in spite of all this, you only care about one question, the one sleeping in your throat: "Will I be cleared to adopt a child?"

I-600A

One of many immigration forms needed by the United States government. Welcome to a dark labyrinth of paperwork. You'll need a ball of golden thread to retrace your way out into the sunshine again. The I–600A is a key that will allow your child to enter the country. You will feel like a mythical hero for obtaining this piece of paper. Theseus has nothing on you.

Life Book

A guidebook to the past. A collection of photographs that tells a story. Especially useful for young children. Photos of the birth country, city, orphanage, caretakers, and even the airplane that carried them to their new home all help the adopted child see their point of origin. An explanation of how they arrived into the present moment. Everyone wants to know where they came from, and these photos are little signposts; they are glowing arrows in the dark.

Match

After months or years of waiting, you suddenly have a dossier of the child you will raise. You might be at work when this email appears. If this happens, you will close your office door, click on the photo, and realize you are looking at your son for the very first time. You will make copies of this photo. You will dash home to your wife, smiling and quaking. Champagne will fizz in the chambers of your heart.

Mother

Origin. Center of gravity. Source. Foundation. Beginning. A woman who shelters a child inside the globe of her body; a woman who cares for a child when the umbilical cord is cut. In the tangled world of adoption there are three types of mothers:

(1) *Birth Mother:* A woman who carries a child in her womb for nine months and then gives up her baby in the hopes it will have a better life elsewhere. Her heart is swaddled in loss. Sorrow fills her veins. This newborn, which lived in her womb, can now only live in her imagination. As the child grows into adulthood, the birth

mother becomes a ghostly presence—both there and not there. She is an opaque star that cannot be seen, but whose gravity is felt. A point of opening and closing. A carrier of secrets, the birth mother wonders what might have been.

(2) *Foster Mother*: A link between the birth mother and the adoptive mother. A woman who raises a child until a home can be found. A legal guardian. For a period of time, the center of a child's universe.

(3) *Adoptive Mother* (also called a *Life Mother*): A woman who cares for a child until she is dead. Proof that love is more powerful than genetics. This woman is a celebrator of birthdays, a giver of language, a dispenser of bandages. Forehead kisser. Cook. Peeler of onions. Assembler of hot dogs, brownies, and warmth. The soft voice and the stern finger. Diaper changer. The saver of college tuition and the maker of Halloween costumes. Scrapbook creator. Santa Claus. The Easter Bunny. Magician. Juggler. Keeper of boundless care. Worrier. Giver. Teacher. Coach. Practitioner of patience. Someone who spends years raising a child in the hopes that child may leave the house and be happy. Like all mothers, she may not be appreciated until she is gone.

Open/Closed

Types of adoption. In the former, the birth parents know who is raising their child and may visit or write letters; in the latter, the birth parents do not know who is raising their child and, in most cases, have no idea where their child is living. At eighteen, the adopted child has access to any photos, information, and/or letters that may have been placed with the Agency (see "Reunion Search"). Most International Adoptions are closed.

An ocean of question marks rises up between the birth country and the adopted country. The opposing shores often feel unswimable to the adult adoptee. They may look out to sea, their mouths closed.

Orphan

A child whose parents have died; also, a child who has been given up for socio-economic reasons; often brought upon by war, pestilence, or natural disaster. Hopefully, a temporary situation. Orphans are left outside police stations in Delhi, given up to nuns in Haiti, or they are sometimes put into a basket and sent down the Nile where they are adopted by an Egyptian princess.

Paternity

A man's bloodline; a chain of genealogy that can offer identity or (in the case of some cultures) banishment, especially if a child is born out of wedlock. Lineage. Pedigree. The genetic material that comes from the testes and *vas deferens*. Sperm corkscrewing into the future; a new branch of the family tree. Note the difference between "Father" and "Daddy".

For most adoptees, their biological father may never be known. He lives on the edge of the crowd, faceless and blurry. His likes, dislikes, and occupation remain a mystery. He may not even know the child exists. Also called a Birth Father, he is a tracing of the chin or the arc of an eyebrow. He hides in the face—both there and not there. A phantom.

See also: *Adoptive Father*. Although his DNA may not be in the child, his love surrounds and frets. Daddy. Dad. Papa. The Old Man. He may not say it as much as he should, but his love is boundless; it overwhelms him; he dreams of carrying his son forever on his shoulders. An adoptive father is a man who does not care about paternity, but does care about being paternal. To be an adoptive father is to take in a child that is not your own and love them as your own. An ancient practice. For Christians, the most famous adoptive father is Joseph the carpenter.

Reunion Search

If the adoption is closed, a child cannot access information about their birth parents until they are eighteen. At this time, they are given any letters or photos the birth mother may have left at the agency; the adult adoptee can now meet their birth mother.

A cocoon webs the heart. Airplanes are boarded. The past and the present meet. Tears are shed. Adoptive parents should stand aside and watch their child be embraced by a woman who made their intertwined lives possible. In the case of Korean adoptions, whisper *kamsahamnida* over and over again. Do not expect a Reunion Search to answer questions. If anything, it will only raise new ones.

Surrender Papers

What happens when a birth mother signs a document and kisses her child goodbye. Blood has been separated by ink. It is a moment that can never be reversed or forgotten. It is a wound that cannot heal.

Trans-

As in "transracial" and "transcultural". It implies movement but it involves transition and transfer. Transformation occurs in both the child and the parents. Adoption is always trans-parent; never transparent.

Waiting Child

A child not yet placed with a family, often due to medical issues. The older the child, the more unlikely it is they will be adopted. Days tick by as they wait to be chosen. They linger. They remain. Their childhood is an ellipsis.

What, When, Why, Where, How

The hinges upon which all questions ride.

Zygote

What all of us once were. A frothing of life.

Letter to His Foster Parents

Dear   ,

I write this without knowing much about you, but since you took such wonderful care of our son in the first year of his life, you need to know how indebted we are to you. Even that word "indebted" is too small. Saying "thank you" is too small. Words are too small to contain the deep appreciation my wife and I feel for your generosity. Not many people would take in an infant and raise them with love, only to then place them onto an airplane a few months later. When you said goodbye to Min-gyu you didn't know where he was going or who was about to love him.

When we picked him up at the Omaha airport (it's a city in the middle of the United States) he was crying and he clearly wanted you, his foster parents. We could tell how attached he was to you and that he was taken care of beautifully in the first few months of his life. The more we interacted with him, the more we knew that he had been raised in a family that loved him. We often think about how hard it must have been to drop him off at the airport and say goodbye.

You should know that we love him deeply and profoundly. He is surrounded by a large loving family and we enjoy playing in the garden with him. His first name is now Sean, and his middle name is Min-gyu because we want to honor his Korean heritage. He is a healthy little boy who loves books, trucks, dinosaurs, chocolate, and running around. We are so very grateful for the life you gave him and, as he grows up, we want him to understand how well he was cared for in his birth country.

My wife and I have enclosed several photos of Sean's first year in America. We cannot imagine our life without him, and we look forward to the grand adventure of raising him.

Thank you. You are a part of his life and we think about your kindness every single day. You made an enormous difference in his life and he was very lucky to have been raised, however temporarily, in your wonderful home.

With all good wishes, blessings, and our heartfelt thanks,

Patrick & Tania Hicks

Afternoon

His First Home

After he was pulled into this world
at 10:51, on an evening in May 2009,

the umbilical cord that tethered him
was snipped.
                              What was I doing,
fourteen hours behind this beginning?

The universe did not flutter my blood,
nor did I feel a shift in my life.

On that morning, I probably sipped coffee
and hunched into the belly of a poem.

Reading his Birth Report two years later

> *height, weight, hepatitis shot,*
> *gender, eye color, blood type,*
> *vaginal birth, physician unknown*

what catches my eye is the gap

between when he burrowed into this world,
and when he was given to an orphanage.

In these missing hours, I imagine his birth mother
cupping the grapefruit softness of his head.

She breathes in his scent,
kisses his nose, memorizes

the topography of his face.
And then, reluctantly,

she lets him go.

His Second Home

After that, someone drove him
through a forest of green traffic lights,
to an orphanage where he was filed in a crib.

His name was written on the side: K2009–0439.
In this depot of the sleeping and wailing,
who held him when he stirred?

At night, did the orphanage director
step into the lighted doorway,
his molasses shadow spilling onto the tiles?

And when my boy wept for milk,
did a young woman fit a bottle
into the drain of his mouth?

Her smile is a slice of moonlight
as he nuzzles into this warehouse
of the lost, who have yet to be found.

Flutter

Beyond the dark rolling Pacific,
across a rind of time zones,
over deserts and fields of corn seed,

in fact, on the other side of the world,

my wife sits up. A strangeness
has butterflied into her nerve endings.

We are at the theatre, watching a play,
and her whisper is hot against my earlobe.

              "He was born today."

My face becomes a question mark.

              "No, really. I can *feel* it."

When we get home,
she marks the calendar with a dot.

It turns out she was right,
but we wouldn't know this for months.

Somehow, beyond all reason,
beyond the arcing vastness of a planet,

my wife felt something—a flutter—
which cannot be explained or denied.

This dot hangs on our calendar,
it is a pinprick of something much larger,

the beginning, perhaps, of a universe

              •

Hide-and-Seek

Sometimes, when you're sleeping,
and the furnace purrs against winter,
I wonder if we did the right thing,
taking you away from Korea.

At the heart of every adoption
is a ripping, a knifepoint, a breaking apart,
      like cracking open an oyster.

When you snore at midnight,
I think of your other possible lives
with a family in Stockholm or London.
You could have been raised near the sea,
or at the foot of a volcano.

But instead, you got us.

Did we do the right thing,
importing you to the other side of the world,
bringing you to the prairie and the ice?

As your bones push into the future,
and the netting of your heart widens,
you will jigsaw these truths into a mirror.

Your family past, so unknown, will make you
      feel snapped. Broken.

                                Exiled.

But until then, I have to tell you
how much I love playing hide-and-seek,
how you run into a bedroom, looking
for me under a quilt,

in a wardrobe,

        how you peek into a closet,
searching here and there for your father.

And when you find me,
it is like a lock clicking open.

Today, the truth is just child's play—
all you have to do is count to ten,
and open your eyes.

"Again," you shout. "Again!"

And so I hide. I wait in the dark,
like an easy answer.

I Believe

my son came into the world halfway around it,
and although the cherry blossoms of Cheongju
aren't in his memory, they fall through his subconscious,
filtering his vision, carpeting the long path ahead. I believe

one day he will stroll through the streets of his ancestors,
their ghostly footfalls crowding around him in curiosity,
and one night he will lay his head on a pillow to fall asleep
beneath a Korean moon for the first time, in years. I believe

when he does this, with the tang of kimchee on his lips,
he will follow the tripwires of imagination back across
the ocean where he'll dream of his British mother,
and, when he does this, he might cry. I believe

he will be confused and lost in the land of his birth,
but the stories we taught him may nourish him along the way—
he might ball up his fists, his mind a hive of honey and venom
as he listens to the murmur of traffic below. I believe

he will get out of bed, look out the hotel window
at the glittering lights of a city that is both his and not his,
and, in this moment of birthright, his vision might water
as a million lights become a river of stars. I believe

he will touch the glass, spread his fingers wide,
and wonder if his birth mother is out there,
if she can feel that her boy—her flesh—
is back home among the cherry blossoms. I believe

my son is strong and good and wise
and that one day he will reconcile his life in America
with his first life, here, in South Korea.
Look now, the future is spread at his feet,

it is a galaxy widening before him.

Surprising Things He Has Said

[holding a flashlight]: Look, Daddy! Me driving the sun!

I have a dead spider in my pocket. See?

Don't touch volcanoes. They're very hot. Like ovens.

Do they have jails in heaven?

[pointing to a light switch]: It's too bright in here. I'm turning on the dark.

[Me]: You're a handsome boy. The chicks are going to dig you when you're older.
[Sean]: Chickens will bury me? Me no want to be buried by chickens.

You are a bad Daddy!
I eat your voice box. Now you not talk to me anymore.

Food in. Poop out.

Dogs aren't human.

Cows eat hay.

Spiders have lots of eyeballs.

That duck by himself. Maybe he lonely? *Hi duck!* Can we stay here and keep him company? That way he not be lonely anymore. We be friends with him. *Hi duck!*

[after trying pumpkin pie]: This is terrible.

Dinosaurs don't go to the dentist. They might poop in the chair.

Brushing my teeth is like a car wash for my mouth.

Only superheroes can punch people.

Don't take the shortcut. Take the longcut.

A cemetery is where dead people live.

[My wife, exasperated]: Hurry up and finish your dinner.
[Sean]: No, I'm going the speed limit, Mommy.

If God is in heaven, does that mean he's dead?

Flashlights can see in the dark.

Me not from Korea.
Me not from America.
Me from home.

Summer in January

If my wife ever started a business
that's what she'd call it:
           "Summer in January".

Suspended downstairs,
in little jugs of time,
is a whole fruit tree.

Each glass jar is sealed

           waiting

to be foomped open,
fork stuck in,
           thick juice of peach
slicking off a plump wedge.

If you close your eyes
there is the taste
           of sunlight and bees
even as snow twirls off the roof,
the thermometer sinks,
and icicles dagger the fence—

the peach tree,
           naked and shivering,
watches the chewing
of the husband inside.

He licks his lips
and dunks his finger
           back into the sweetness

           again

                 and again.

Read This

and imagine how it came
into your hands.

Riding the glide
of undreamed words, my pencil skates
through a February night.

Outside the window,
snow confettis through a streetlight,
it falls like words onto a page.

I roll around, make snow angels,
hold out my tongue—

I think of water and evolution,
but I do not write of these things.

Later, I reach for a stamp,
and address this artifact of time
to an editor.

She sees something, life perhaps,
and my poem is clustered

in the land of this book.
It exists here, on page 54.

And then somehow,
(miracle of miracles),
it climbs onto your shore,

shakes water from its damp fur,
and, as the droplets arc into the sun,
you imagine snow floating

through a streetlight,
and you live, for a moment,
in the distant world of a stranger.

At Pollock's Toy Museum

London, England

The tin soldiers and golliwogs disturb me,
so too does a puppet of Hitler.

The children who owned these dolls,
these miniature trains, these wooden horses

and jacks, from the days of Shakespeare,
are all gone.

An Egyptian sparrow,
made of clay,

is in the corner,
its wing snapped off

sometime in the last 40 centuries.
It was found near a mummy,

but a girl once loved it,
she fed it imaginary grain,

and tucked it away,
deep inside the safety

of her pocket.

Watching My Mother Take Care of My Son is a Form of Time Travel

It is 1970 again, the cold war is hot,
      and my mother mashes corn with a fork.
Sergeant Pepper floats around the house
      as I sit in the corner, spying on my past.

The woman who carried me into this world
      now feeds my son—the spoon between them
is a pendulum swinging from one generation
      to the next, marking time against a bowl.

My boy won't remember any of this,
      but one day he might read this poem
and travel back in time. If he thinks about 1970,
      he might see me drooling in a highchair.

On television, Vietnam foams with napalm,
      Apollo rumbles like a dart towards the moon,
hundreds of meals are spooned into me,
      and the earth continues its blessed spin.

It makes me think back to World War II.
      My mother is a baby in Northern Ireland—
the Nazis are busy dynamiting synagogues,
      and turning families into ash.

My grandmother lifts a spoon of honeyed oatmeal,
      taps my mother's nose, and thinks back to 1915—
back to when she was fed beneath hissing gas lamps,
      and the Kaiser's Zeppelins swam across the sky.

These stories shaped me, and they will shape my boy,
    even though he came from beyond me.
Hiding in his veins are fishing villages, rice paddies,
    and the slashing knife of the Korean War.

If I go back to 1953, I see a woman in a *hanbok*,
    maybe she crouches near a blown out tank,
maybe she feeds peaches and honey to a girl,
    maybe this girl is somehow linked to my boy?

My son laughs in the 21st-century, and I look up.
    The spoon pendulums between he and my mother.
I see now that memory is a crumbling honeycomb,
    in order for it to survive, it must first be fed.

The Last Time I Spoke to My Grandfather

His heart was a slit drum,
the valves ragged and slack.
This symbol of love and courage,
which for years had rocked inside its bony cage,
was on the verge of slowing down,

stopping.

I pushed his wheelchair into the sun,
and we talked of his home in Belfast,
of the Titanic, and of IRA bombs
blasting jagged steel into bone.

Already in the midnight of mourning,
I put on the wheel-brake,
and kneeled down before him.

"Thanks for what you put in the will," I said.
"We're going to adopt a little boy with it when . . ."

A smile lifted his face. "Good. Say hello to him.
Tell him I wish we could have met."

And then, slowly, on a beautiful spring day,
one swollen with the promise of life,
I pushed my grandfather back into the hospice.

The Inventor of the Car Bomb

—thinking of my old life in Northern Ireland

It goes like this:

pack Semtex around a fuse,
latch the trunk shut, carefully,
then park beside a soft target—
this is the hardest part,
which is made easier over time.
The last step is to stroll away,
hands in your pockets.

Glass and rubble will hail down
onto a spray of blood and ribcage.
The plumage of oily smoke
will geyser up from torn metal.
Burning tires, those hellfire halos,
will flame around the ripped carcass of a Ford.
Then, silence, as the ambulance whines awake.

Someone was the first to do this
and now, every day, they pop all over the world,
they detonate inside my television.
The car bomb was perfected in Northern Ireland,
and I know the man who nightmared it up.
He showed the world how it could be made into a virus,
an epidemic of explosions, a daily shattering.

Tall and lean, he's a peace activist now.
In Derry, he holds his Guinness to mine—*Sláinte*—
and we drink in the black stout. We lick our lips
and talk about how peace, quiet peace,
has finally found Northern Ireland.

We leave the pub waltzing on booze,
and Liam points us down a moonslick street.
There is an empty van beside us.
He tells me exactly how much Semtex
can be packed into the back.

When we move away,
our feet click off the concrete like a timer.

The Poet Laureate of North Korea

She waits for the words,

but her journal is as empty
as her stomach.

The paper beneath her fist
is a snowy field of hunger.

She wants to write about sunsets
that look like bullet wounds,

birds that can't migrate south,
and the vanishing of her father.

She sits with a pen,
microphones spying on the silence.

When she begins to write,
it is like a rake sinking into the soil.

Nightfall

Adoptable

If a doctor hadn't clicked open a pen
          and scrawled nine letters
                    onto a medical chart,

my son wouldn't be here today.
I write it out now in celebration.

          A d o p t a b l e

I imagine this man, Dr. Jeong,
          with coffee on his breath,

turning my son over
and over.
                    He listens

to the hummingbird of a heartbeat,
and squints into a toothless yowl.

Perhaps there is a grunt of approval,
as casual as if he were testing a cantaloupe
or picking persimmons at a market.

Almost on impulse, quick as a signature,
                    he splashes out a lone word

that sets an entire life into motion.

Adoptable labeled my son,
it created a passport and baggage,
it revved the engines of a 747.

Adoptable is now my blood and my song—
it is tattooed onto my tongue.

The Birth Mothers

They amble through shopping malls
and neon-splashed streets.

They laugh into glowing cell phones,
ride commuter trains in Seoul, and needle
their way through tangled lanes.

They lock memory in a box.

They might touch their bellies,
and remember a ghost
that once billowed inside them.

These women do not tell their husbands
that, once, back when they were sixteen,
they gave birth to a boy.

All of Korea groans under guilt—
such a wealthy nation, and yet
innocent illegitimates are not welcome.

The bloodline must remain pure.

And so these mothers of the missing
stream through their days not thinking
about a face that has tumbled into fog.

But near the end,
on their clammy deathbeds,
do they whisper the name of their firstborn?

Do they weep for this child
that has slipped through their fingers?

Do they tell their adult children
about this secret they have carried for decades,
this unspoken name buried in their throats?

"Listen," they might say,
        breathing out the hidden words at last,

"You have a brother in America. Find him.
        Tell him, I never forgot he was mine."

Ghost

I think of you,
sometimes

but mostly,
you are as noticeable
as a blink.

According to the Birth Report,
you don't know about my son.

      (Your son.)

But I think of you
when I study the contour of his nose.

I see your ghost flickering
in his face.

Birth father,
I don't know your name,
but maybe you're in college now.

Maybe you're in Seoul,
wolfing down *ddukbokkie*
before you run off

to a dance club,
your body flickering
beneath strobe lights—

    appearing
  disappearing

    appearing
  disappearing

much as you do,
in my unsaid thoughts.

Looking Up at the Stars While My Son Plays with a Toy

—August 25, 2012

When I think of Voyager, I am in awe that this webbing of metal, no larger than a car, is leaving our solar system today. It is a bottle tossed out into a vast ocean of darkness. Godspeed, you little poem. Godspeed for the uncharted territory ahead.

Story Time

Fresh in superhero pajamas,
you drop into my lap and open books
as if they were butterflies.

You point at pineapples, tigers,
scuba divers, outriggers, mandibles,
and ostriches, asking for words.

You have trouble with
ankylosaurus and pteranodon.
T-Rex and stegosaurus come easily.

Protocolepiocephale is hard on us both.

You roll these doughy syllables
on your tongue,
            kneading their taste.

I love how you open an atlas
and point at England or Ireland.

"This my country," you say, stabbing
the Korean peninsula. Then your fingers hike

across the blue puddle of the Pacific—
just an easy stroll between
South Korea and South Dakota.

With all these books fluttering around us,
it feels like the whole world is blossoming open,
that life itself is winging up from the floor.

That's when you point at a meteor—
            a fireball that will punch the earth
            and turn dinosaurs into bone.

You turn the page,
and look at the timber of their fossils.

"Why do things die?" you ask.

I think of the hive inside your head,
and the spark that jolts your heart.

I look at the empty books around us,
and silently demand an answer
from whichever god that authored us.

Delicate

Delicate are the tendons that glide beneath our skin.
Delicate are the neurons that spark memory.

Delicate is the hammer—and the drum—inside our ears.
Delicate is the heart that accordions a lifetime of blood.

Delicate are the scars that whisper our past.
Delicate is the moonlight, floating upon a lake.

Delicate are the seasons that age our bodies,
and the billion suns that shine above us at night.

Delicate is the birdsong of traffic,
and the watery gears of our bodies.

Delicate is the candle,
    delicate the flinching flame.

Delicate is the fingertip,
waiting to turn a page.

Delicate is this book in your hands,
the dried ink on this page, the topography
between author and reader.

It is understanding that each second, each breath,
each ballooning of our lungs, is just a wisp of air,

as easily finished as a poem.

When He is an Old Man

Long after my body has been turned into ash,
and his own children have walked into middle-age,
they will eventually gather around his hospital bed.
My son, an old man with papery skin,
will be hooked up to an octopus of machines.
Tubes will push fluid into his body—
his ribcage will rise and fall. His heart will blip.

He might be scared, but also content
with the arc and burn of his life.
I will stand at the foot of his bed
just as I did when he was a baby,
                    watching him breathe.

As nurses rush in for his final moments,
I'd like to put my cool hand on his cheek,
and whisper into his ear that his daddy still loves him.
If there is another life, I'll be waiting for him
just as I did at the Omaha airport when we first met.
I'll be the one craning my neck at the new arrivals,
waving my hands like crazy, ecstatic at last
                    to welcome him home.

PREVIOUS PRAISE FOR PATRICK HICKS

"In The Commandant of Lubizec, *Patrick Hicks imagines the unimaginable and thus gives us a glimpse into the terrible complexity of the human heart. This is a fascinating and important book."*
ROBERT OLEN BUTLER, winner of the Pulitzer Prize

"This is a vividly detailed, terrifying, convincing, and completely spellbinding story rooted in those murderous events we now call the Holocaust. [. . .] Patrick Hicks has accomplished a very difficult literary task. He has given a believable and fresh and original face to barbarism. What a fine book this is."
TIM O'BRIEN, author of *The Things They Carried,* winner of the National Book Award

"The Commandant of Lubizec *melds the historian's factual precision with a storyteller's compassion and love for humanity. This is fiction at its highest register—creating inroads into the past so that we might hear those murdered in the extermination camps of the Holocaust, so that we might better recognize the world we have inherited. Profound and trenchant,* The Commandant of Lubizec *is a brave and unflinching book. It is a stunning literary debut. I urge you to read it before it's made into a film."*
BRIAN TURNER, author of *Here, Bullet* and *Phantom Noise*

"A heart-rending novel about a Nazi death camp that didn't exist—but could have. Hicks' prose is clear and unflinching [. . .] Thought-provoking and gut-wrenchingly powerful."
KIRKUS REVIEWS

"The fictional presentation here measures up to any factual account of the Holocaust this reviewer has ever read. Highly recommended, especially for general readers who wish to know more about this unspeakable chapter of human history. Even specialists will be taken in by its human-interest dimension."
LIBRARY JOURNAL

"Out of the cooling ashes of Holocaust history, Patrick Hicks manages to break our hearts with a story we thought we already knew. The Commandant of Lubizec is profound, provocative, and profane in all the best ways. While reading The Commandant of Lubizec, one question kept running through my mind: 'Was it really this bad?' Through his all-too-real fiction, Patrick Hicks convinces me that, sadly, the answer is 'Yes.' The Commandant of Lubizec is important and unforgettable."

DAVID ABRAMS, author of Fobbit

"A book of poems about London by any non-Londoner has to be of interest. But a book of poems about London by a 'foreigner' has to be of especial interest [. . .] with his clear-eyed perception and the ability to focus on the apposite and illuminating details he has something of Chaucer's and Defoe's gift in his writing."

ACUMEN

"Patrick Hicks writes poems of personal history, social history, world history. It is, I think, his way of redrawing the map of our human hearts."

RICHARD JONES, author of A Perfect Time and The Blessing

"These finely wrought lyrics are focused on the family—in Ireland, Canada, the United States, and in-transit—to reveal origins, maps, anxieties, and coincidences. Hicks recovers from time desires, loves, and the moist mother tongues of the dispersed. Traveling Through History is a singularly impressive first collection—allusive, engaging, exciting."

EAMONN WALL, author of A Tour of Your Country and Writing the Irish West

PATRICK HICKS is the author of seven books, including *The Commandant of Lubizec*, *This London*, and *Finding the Gossamer*. His work has appeared in some of the most vital literary journals in America, including *Ploughshares*, *Glimmer Train*, *The Missouri Review*, *Prairie Schooner*, and many others. He has been nominated seven times for the Pushcart Prize, been a finalist for the High Plains Book Award, and also the Gival Press Novel Award. He has won the *Glimmer Train* Fiction Award as well as a number of grants, including ones from the Bush Artist Foundation and the National Endowment for the Humanities. He is the Writer-in-Residence at Augustana College and also a faculty member at the MFA program at Sierra Nevada College. His first collection of short stories, *The Collector of Names*, is forthcoming with Schaffner Press.